Edinburgh
A Capital Story

Frances and Gordon Jarvie

Illustrated by Heather Nevay

Chambers

Cramond fort.

Beginnings

AD 190 Almost two thousand years ago, the Roman armies were busy colonising Britain, building their famous camps, towns, roads and fortifications, and turning the British peoples into citizens of Rome. The northern boundary of their direct rule was the Antonine Wall (built around AD 145), stretching between the Forth and Clyde estuaries.

The Romans had built Dere Street up from Newcastle to the Forth, through Lauderdale and over Soutra. Their destination was the outpost of Cramond, their fort at the mouth of the Almond, an eastern defence for the Antonine Wall. At Cramond the Romans had a harbour and anchorage, and excavation is slowly uncovering more and more remains; fort, ramparts, ditches, workshops, residences, granaries and bath-houses.

Read *The Boy with the Bronze Axe* by Kathleen Fidler for a fictional idea of life at this time.

AD 638 Five hundred years later, the Castle is said to have boasted a Great Hall where the warriors of King Mynyddog feasted. He was one of Dunedin's most famous ancient chiefs. One can imagine that at this time the Castle Rock was becoming a prime defensive site.

Dunedin.

The Romans had long since retreated to defend their Empire nearer home, and the Votadini were now overwhelmed by the Anglian kingdom of Northumbria to the south. In time the Forth estuary became the boundary with the Pictish-Scottish kingdom to the north. The site of Edinburgh was of growing strategic importance.

AD 1093 By this date there was probably a large cluster of houses on the ridge directly east of the Castle, huddled close for protection in time of danger. By this time too, the Scots king Malcolm Canmore and his queen, Margaret, had made Edinburgh Castle their home, and it is from this time that Queen Margaret's Chapel dates (see page 6).

An artist's impression of the hill fort at Dunsapie on Arthur's Seat. East Lothian forest in the distance.

Edinburgh's Coat of Arms

The arms of the city feature a silver shield, in which is depicted a three towered castle with black stonework, standing on a rocky base.

Above the shield is an eight-pointed gold coronet, with each point representing a thistle. The coronet supports an anchor and cable – the city's Lord Provost also bore the historical title Admiral of the Forth.

Above the anchor is the city's motto in Latin: *Nisi dominus frustra* (Except the Lord in vain). This comes from the book of Psalms 127: Except the Lord build the house, they labour in vain that build it, except the Lord keep the city, the watcher waketh but in vain.

The shield is borne by two supporting figures. On the left is a young woman with long hair. On the right is a female deer or doe. The woman is thought to represent the beauty of the city, or she may be the 'maiden richly clad' – a reference to the *Castrum Puellarum*, or Maiden Castle, referred to on old charters. The doe is thought to have been taken from the reverse of the town's great seal of 1496 which depicted St Giles, the patron saint of the burgh, with his doe or hind.

Edinburgh's coat of arms.

Edinburgh's Patron Saint

It is impossible now to determine why St Giles was chosen long ago as Edinburgh's patron saint. But references to him - in connection with a monastic house and to lands south of the city called St Giles Grange - go back to before A.D. 900. Most Scottish churches of the period were dedicated to Scottish or Irish saints such as Ninian, Mirren, Mungo, Columba or Patrick. St Giles was very popular in France however, where he spent his adult life. His fame as a holy man probably travelled from there to Scotland.

St Giles, or Aegidius, was born in Athens in A.D. 640, of royal descent. He was brought up piously, was well educated and soon became famous as a holy man who performed amazing miracles. As a genuinely humble man, Giles shrank from the role of local celebrity. He decided to leave his native Greece and cross the sea to serve God in a place where he would be unknown. In A.D. 665 he travelled to Arles in the south of France where, once again, he soon became famous. Thereafter he lived as a hermit for many years, later becoming abbot of a monastery near Nimes.

A 15th-century seal of St Giles' Kirk.

Old pictures of the saint usually show him with his hind, or deer. This is a reference to a famous episode in his life. While living as a hermit in the forest near Nimes, St Giles's hind was once threatened with certain death by a large hunting party. She took refuge with her master in the thickest part of the forest. Arrows were fired into the thicket, one wounding the saint. When the hunters found St Giles bleeding, with his hind crouching unharmed at his feet, they were filled with guilt and remorse, and eventually built a monastery there.

The High Kirk of Edinburgh was dedicated to St Giles in 1243, since when he has been the burgh's patron saint. St Giles is also the patron saint of cripples and beggars.

Edinburgh Castle

Edinburgh Castle.

Edinburgh Castle has to be the starting point for any description of the city. It provides the best bird's eye view of the modern city, and it is the place where the recorded history of Edinburgh begins.

The Castle Rock is a natural site for a fort, and there has been a settlement here for over two thousand years. With steep rocks on three sides, and clear views in all directions, it would have been a perfect vantage point from which to observe the progress of Viking longboats sailing up the Forth, or armies approaching by land.

Today the Castle is approached from the Esplanade, the parade ground where you can occasionally see the Changing of the Guard ceremony or, during the Festival, watch the Military Tattoo. Cross the old (dry) Moat by the Drawbridge. The niches on either side of the entrance display bronze statues of Sir William Wallace and King Robert the Bruce, two of Scotland's national heroes. The Gatehouse is modern (1887), built as an entrance worthy of the Castle rather than a true fortification.

The approach road climbs to the Portcullis Gate beneath the State Prison with its enormously thick medieval walls - 3.5 to 5 m thick. This was the original entrance to the Castle, erected by David II about 1358. Through this gate to the left are the Lang Stairs, the main medieval approach to the Castle.

At the top of the Lang Stairs, to the right, is one of the oldest buildings in Edinburgh - St Margaret's Chapel. It was built in A.D. 1080, by Queen Margaret, wife of Malcolm Canmore. King Malcolm was the son of King Duncan, killed by Macbeth (as told in Shakespeare's play). St Margaret's Chapel is a tiny building (the interior is less than 6 m by 4 m), still used occasionally for weddings and other services.

Another interesting building is the Palace, where several of the medieval kings of Scotland lived. Here you will see the small room in which Mary Queen of Scots gave birth to the future king James VI of Scotland and I of England. Here too is the Crown Room, the vaulted strongroom containing 'the honours of Scotland' – the crown, orb, sceptre and sword of state of the kings of Scotland.

Next to the Palace is the Old Parliament Hall, or Great Hall, where the Scots Parliament met from the 14th century till as late as 1640. The Hall was also used by James IV and later kings for state ceremonial occasions. There is a fine, open-timbered hammerbeam roof and a display of arms and armour on the walls.

Facing the Great Hall across Crown Square is an imposing modern building – the Scottish National War Memorial. It was opened in 1927, and contains galleries of honour with fine stained glass windows. It is a national shrine in remembrance of the dead of both world wars.

Completing Crown Square is the Scottish United Services Museum, an interesting collection of military relics, uniforms, and trophies of the Scottish regiments through the ages – and a reminder that Edinburgh Castle is still a working military barracks. The vaults under the Museum are known as the French Prisons, recalling their use to house French prisoners of war in the Napoleonic conflicts. Also now housed here is Mons Meg, the massive siege cannon (struck at Mons in Belgium in 1486) which used to stand on the Half-Moon Battery overlooking the city.

Finally, no visit to the Castle is complete without a visit to the Half-Moon Battery to admire the magnificent view of the city and to inspect the cannon. The 1 o'clock gun is fired from the nearby Argyll Battery each weekday, a ceremony established in 1851. The noise of the gun can be heard all over the town. It makes visitors jump, pigeons fly about in alarm, and it makes local people check their watches.

(Also read about Edinburgh Castle in *Scottish Castles* and *Scottish Heroes and Heroines of Long Ago*, both in the *Otter* series.)

Castle gate, with the statues of King Robert the Bruce and Sir William Wallace.

Map of Edinburgh Castle.

1. Esplanade.
2. Half moon Battery.
3. Scottish National War Memorial.
4. Crown Square.
5. Portcullis gate.
6. Saint Margaret's Chapel.

Holyroodhouse

Holyrood was the name given to the abbey founded in 1128 by King David I after a hunting accident in the royal parks around Arthur's Seat. In those days, thick forest covered much of the area - the name Salisbury Crags, bare enough of trees today, came from 'sallies brae' (willowtree hill). King David was hunting a stag in the forest, when it turned on him, knocked him from his horse and threatened to kill him with its massive antlers. Miraculously, a cross appeared in the King's hands, with which he contrived to defend himself. Grateful to God for delivering him, the King gave land to the canons of St Augustine, ordering them to establish there a church of the Holy Rood (or Cross). The abbey prospered, and there was a guest house for royal visitors from its earliest years.

In due course, the canons of the abbey gave their name to the burgh of Canongate. The canons' gait was the canons' road which led up to the High Street of the adjacent burgh of Edinburgh.

In 1500, King James IV built the North West Tower of the present palace, transforming the abbey guest house into a building fit for a king. The matching South West Tower was built for Charles II in the 1670s, when much of the rest of the palace was completed in the style of Louis XIV. It was on the second floor of the North West Tower that Mary Queen of Scots had her bedchamber, and most of the original furnishings survive. Here David Rizzio, Mary's Italian secretary, was seized by a band of Scottish nobles and stabbed to death in her presence. A brass plate marks the spot where he fell.

Holyroodhouse.

Mary Queen of Scots.

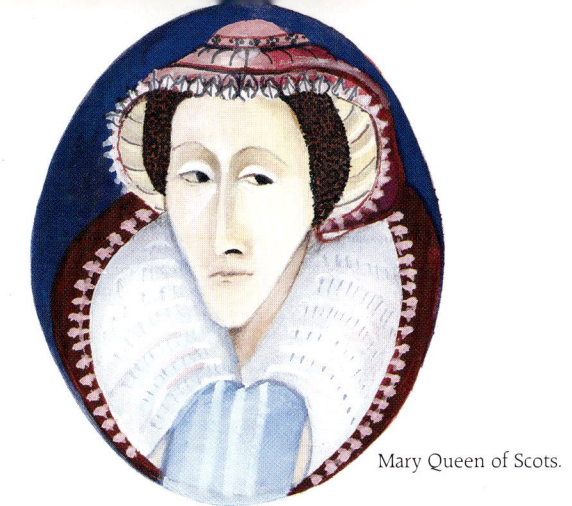

Holyroodhouse has seen stirring and bloody times down the centuries. Burned by the English in 1544, it was a royal dwelling till 1603, when the Court moved to London and James VI of Scotland became James I of England. Holyrood then served as a military headquarters for Cromwell and later for Bonnie Prince Charlie, as well as providing the backcloth for some of George IV's regal functions in 1822 (largely organised by the efforts of Sir Walter Scott). In 1661, the abbey was for four months scene of the final lying-in-state of the great Marquis of Montrose.

Features of the Palace of Holyroodhouse today are the fine Renaissance-style courtyard, the State Rooms, Queen Mary's apartments and the long Picture Gallery, with its portraits of 111 Scottish monarchs. The Dutch artist Jacob de Wit may have had his imagination working overtime as 30 of the kings depicted apparently never existed!

Today the Palace is the official residence of the Queen in Scotland, and is used annually by her and by her representatives at the General Assembly of the Church of Scotland, for state functions, investitures and garden parties. The Palace is closed to visitors when the royal family is in residence.

Unfortunately Holyrood Abbey, adjacent to the Palace, is today in the ruinous state it reached in 1768 when the stone slab roof collapsed.

The ruins of Holyrood Abbey.

The Royal Mile

For hundreds of years, this was Edinburgh's main thoroughfare. It runs today as it did from the beginning in an almost straight line from the Castle downhill to Holyrood. The line of the Royal Mile follows the ridge, or geological tail, which formed east of the Castle's rocky volcanic crag. The original township of Edinburgh spread down this ridge from the Castle, and slightly later the burgh of Canongate spread up the hill from Holyrood to meet it. By 1500 it was continuously built up.

Running off at right angles from the Royal Mile are the countless narrow wynds, closes, vennels, courts and lands which gave the map of the medieval city something of a herring-bone appearance: with the Royal Mile for the spine of the fish.

The buildings and streets of the Royal Mile are a comprehensive history in stone of the Scottish Middle Ages. They witnessed many key events of Scottish history – not just the pomp and ceremony of royal processions and proclamations, but also the darker passions of the Edinburgh mob. But the Royal Mile is more than just a medieval theme park, because so many of its buildings are still in use: here are still the Sheriff Courthouse, the City Chambers, the Scottish supreme courts, the Central Police Station, a teacher training college and brewery offices as well as modern hotels, restaurants and facilities for the visitor.

Many of the vanished landmarks of the Royal Mile are commemorated in the cobbles of the street. (Watch out for the traffic when you look for the following!) The outline of the old city jail or Tolbooth is marked in Parliament Square, as is its gate – a heart-shaped pattern of setts, the 'Heart of Midlothian'. A nearby T-shape marks the site of Edinburgh's last public hanging, in the 1860s. Further down the Royal Mile on the south side, almost at St John Street, a cross of St John is marked on the roadway. This marks the boundary between the two burghs of Edinburgh and Canongate. At the bottom of the Royal Mile you used to see three brass letters SSS (standing for sanctuary) in the roadway. This reminded passers-by that long ago, and even up to the mid 1800s, debtors could find sanctuary from the law in the lands of the Abbey of Holyrood.

The Royal Mile is in fact four streets running into each other. From the Castle Esplanade, they are **Castle Hill**, the **Lawnmarket**, the **High Street** and the **Canongate**. By far the best way to get to know the Royal Mile, and to learn about some of its history, is to walk down it. There is much to see.

Castle Hill leaves the Esplanade with the romantic and brightly-coloured block of Ramsay Garden (1893) on the left. It is by Sir Patrick Geddes, the town planner. Cannonball House (16th-century front), on the right, faces the well-concealed Castlehill Reservoir (1851), on the site of the city's first piped water supply from

Heart of Midlothian.

Comiston Springs (1681), 5 km distant. The Outlook Tower, or Camera Obscura, was also a Patrick Geddes project and is a good vantage point in clear weather. It has a system of lenses like a giant revolving periscope which projects a live moving picture of the city on to a concave white table.

Castle Hill now enters the slightly wider **LAWNMARKET**, or landmarket, where the products of the land were traditionally bought and sold. Gladstone's Land is mentioned on page 180. Milne's Court is interesting as a late 17th-century effort to introduce the spaciousness of a small town square into the cramped closes and wynds of the Old Town. Through Wardrop's Close is Lady Stair's House, now a museum with interesting relics of Scott, Burns and Stevenson. At the corner of Bank Street is Deacon Brodie's Tavern, a reminder that the devious deacon lived opposite (see page 42).

At Parliament Square the Lawnmarket becomes the **HIGH STREET**, the centre of the Old Town. Parliament House was the seat of the Scots Parliament from 1639 to 1707 when it was united with the English Parliament in London. It has a fine ceiling and stained glass windows, and is now the home of the Scottish Supreme Court. St Giles' High Kirk and the Mercat Cross, in many ways the focus of the street, are mentioned further on pages 16 and 39. Almost opposite, on the left, are the City Chambers (1754), one of the few Georgian buildings on the Royal Mile. Further down, on the right, the Tron Kirk (founded 1637) was built for those worshippers who quit St Giles' when King Charles I made the latter an episcopalian cathedral. Its name is from a tron, or weighing machine, that stood on the site. Occasionally open to visitors, you can see the remains of Marlin's Wynd, a 16th-century cobbled close which has been excavated.

Further down, on the left, look out for Paisley's Close, with its dramatic story in stone above the entry: 'Heave awa chaps, I'm no dead yet'. This reminds passers-by of the rescue of a boy trapped in the building when it partially collapsed in the 1860s. Beyond Paisley's Close

Lawnmarket in the 19th century.

are Moubray House (1464, perhaps the oldest house in the street) and John Knox House (see page 36). The street narrows considerably, and here was another feature that has now entirely disappeared: the Netherbow Port, one of the main ports, or gates, of the walled city, demolished in 1764. This gate, with a fine tower and clock above it, was set right across the street. A brass plate now marks its former location. Almost opposite is World's End Close (so called because it was at the city's boundary). St Mary's Street was formerly the first wynd outside the city's walls.

'The Netherbow Port might be called the Temple Bar of Edinburgh: intersecting the High Street at its termination, it divided Edinburgh, properly so called, from the suburb named the Canongate, as Temple Bar separates London from Westminster.'
(Sir Walter Scott, *Heart of Midlothian*.)

After the teeming High Street, the **CANONGATE** was comparatively rural. Rich Scottish nobles built town houses here, to be near the court at Holyroodhouse and away from the squalor of Edinburgh. Examples were Moray House (1625, now a teacher training college), Acheson House (1633, now a craft centre), and Queensberry House (1681, now an old folk's home) – all splendid mansions in their day.

In addition to some fine housing, Canongate also had its own Tolbooth (1591, originally the burgh courthouse and jail, now a museum called The People's Story), its own Dutch-looking parish kirk (1688), and its own mercat cross (now removed to the Canongate kirkyard). White Horse Close at the foot of the street has been well restored, and may have been the royal mews in the 16th century. The White Horse Inn, at the back of this group of buildings, was once the main coaching house for travellers to and from London.

White Horse Close.

Canongate Tolbooth.

Holyrood gates.

The Town Walls

There were three phases in the enclosure of the city - the King's Wall (1450), the Flodden Wall (1514-60) and Telfer's Wall (1628-36). The first merely protected the south side of the High Street down to the Netherbow Port. The Flodden Wall was built after the disastrous defeat of the Scots by the English at the Battle of Flodden Field in 1513 and took the Grassmarket and Cowgate into the protection of the city. The third, Telfer's Wall (named after one of its stonemasons, John Tailefer) enclosed Heriot's Hospital. All these walls were to the south of the Old Town, the Nor' Loch providing a natural defence to the north.

In the Middle Ages, the royal burghs had all sorts of trading privileges, and they defended them jealously. These old fortifications were as much a protection by the city's guilds and incorporated trades against smugglers as a military defence against the English. The gates would also be closed in times of plague.

In some sections, the walls were fortified dwellings (for example, in St Mary's Street) or strengthened garden walls. Some artillery emplacements were added in 1650 and 1715. Demolition started from 1762 and today very little survives. The best remains are in the Pleasance and the Vennel (off the Grassmarket).

The town gates were called ports (from the French for door = *porte*). There are still streets named after two of them - Bristo Port and West Port. The others were Netherbow Port (studs in the High Street mark its position), Cowgate Port, Potterrow Port and New Port. It is worth mentioning that the streets of Canongate and Cowgate do not refer to gates. Gate, or gait, in these words means walk - so the Cowgate was the walk of the cows to and from the Grassmarket where they were bought and sold, and the Canongate was the walk of the canons of Holyrood Abbey.

A cross section of the Old Town to show the location of the walls.

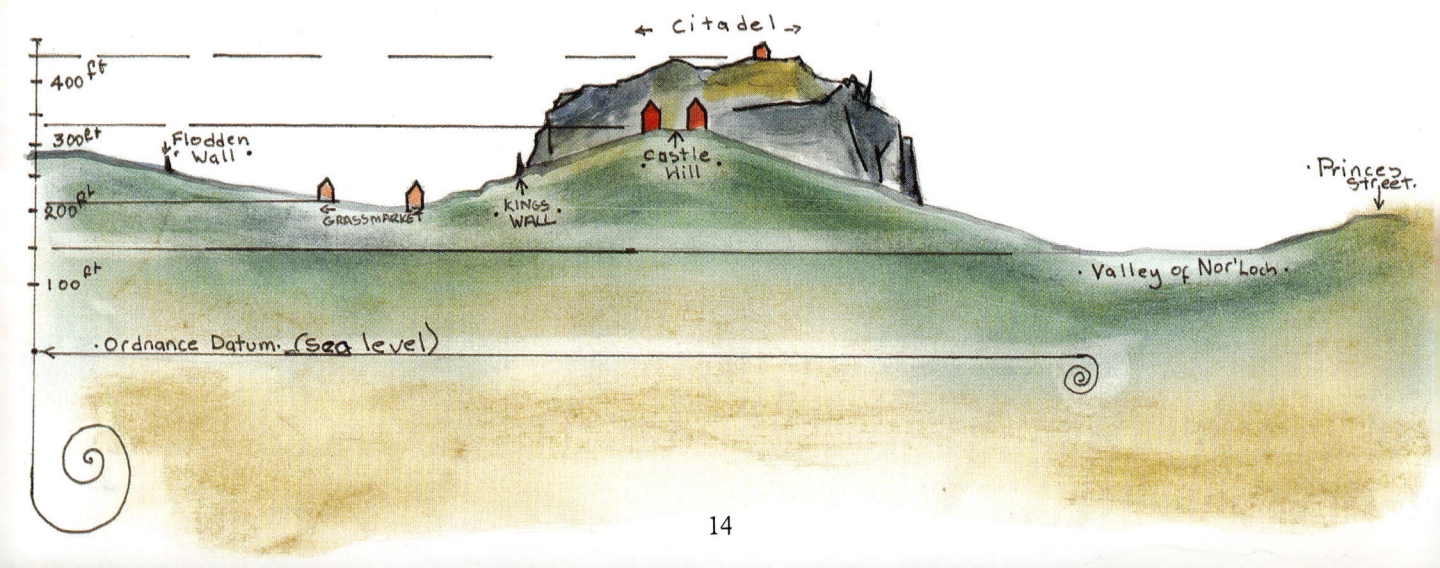

The 'Ancient Royalty' of Edinburgh enclosed within these walls covered an area of 400 m^2. The City of Edinburgh District today covers 169 km^2. To remind yourself just how compact the city once was, follow the line of the walls and take a walk from Johnston Terrace down the steps to the Grassmarket, then up the Vennel to Lauriston Place, then left and continue along Teviot Place, South College Street and Drummond Street, then left again down the Pleasance, St Mary's Street and Jeffrey Street.

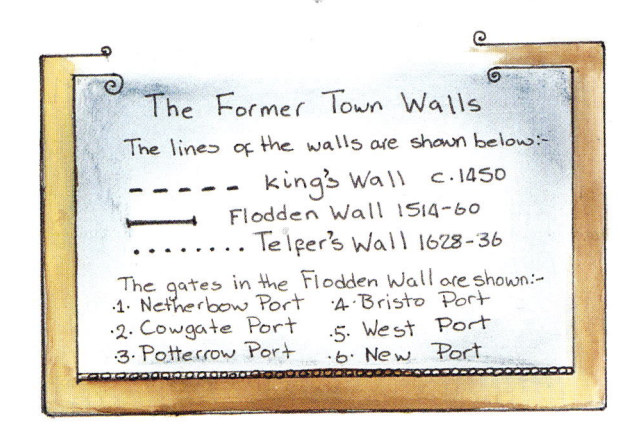

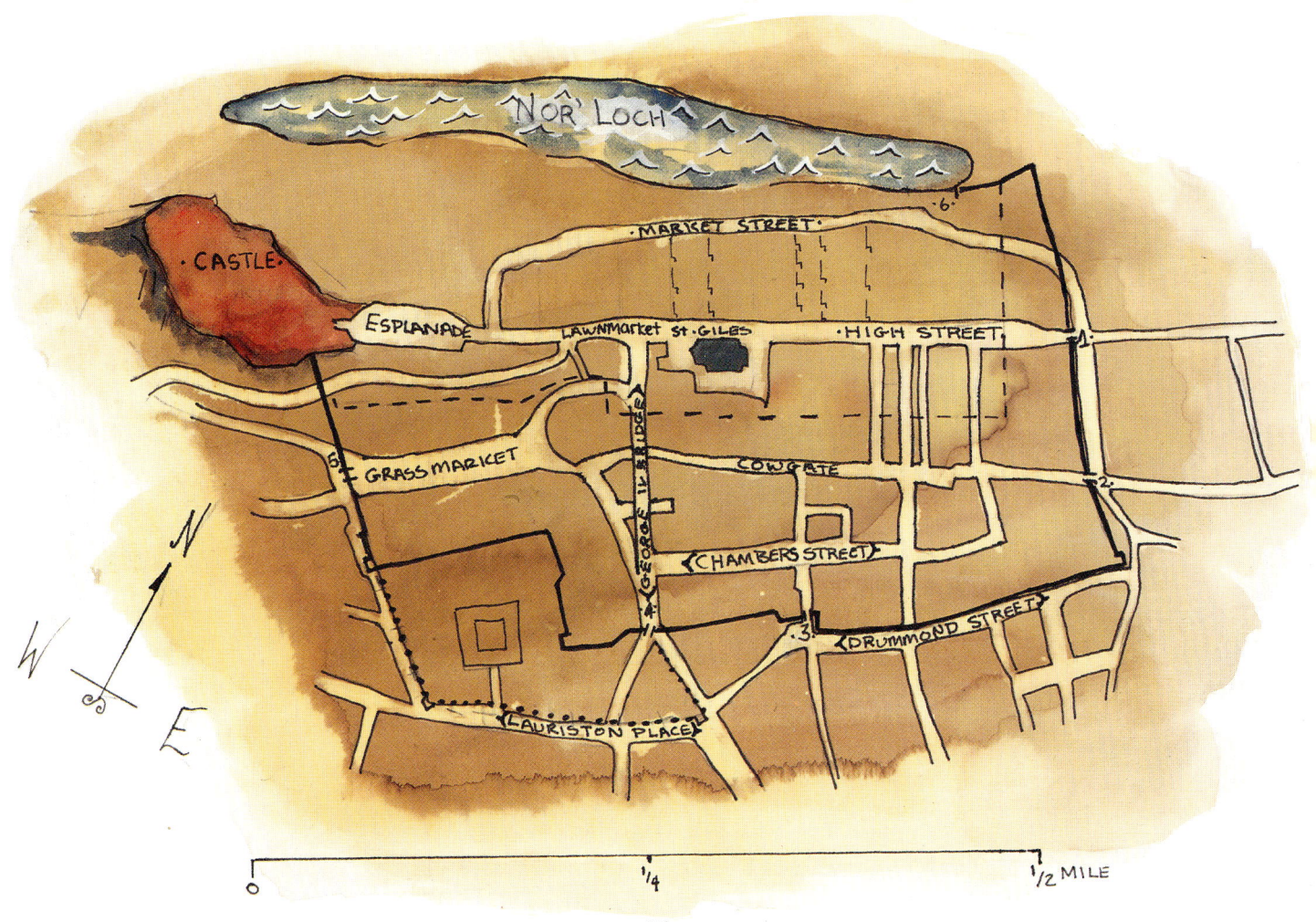

The Former Town Walls

The lines of the walls are shown below:-

- – – – – King's Wall c.1450
- ——— Flodden Wall 1514-60
- .... Telfer's Wall 1628-36

The gates in the Flodden Wall are shown:-
- 1. Netherbow Port
- 2. Cowgate Port
- 3. Potterrow Port
- 4. Bristo Port
- 5. West Port
- 6. New Port

A cross section of St Giles.

St Giles' High Kirk

For many hundreds of years - right up to the time of the Reformation in Scotland (1560) - St Giles' High Kirk was the only parish church in the royal burgh of Edinburgh. So it was a building central to the city's story, centrally located in the Old Town halfway down the Royal Mile. The town and its high kirk were burnt down by the English in 1385. There was also a rather disastrous 'improvement' or restoration of the building in 1828-34, so the present kirk is made up of various re-buildings and extensions.

Many new aisles and chapels were added over the years - St John's Aisle, Albany Aisle, Preston Aisle, Chepman Aisle, Holy Blood Aisle were built between 1395 and 1518. In due course the burgh kirk became vast enough to be divided by stone walls into three separate churches and congregations. These divisions were not finally removed until the late 19th century.

The medieval Choir and the modern Thistle Chapel are features of the interior. The late 15th-century Central Tower and its crown spire have been a striking aspect of the exterior - and of the Edinburgh skyline - for almost 500 years.

St Giles' is often called a cathedral. Strictly speaking, the term only applied for a period of five years - between 1633 and 1638 when it had Protestant Episcopalian bishops. There were no Catholic bishops here before the Reformation, and of course there are no bishops in the Church of Scotland's presbyterian organisation either.

The Crown spire of St Giles.

There is a famous anecdote about St Giles', dating to one of its short periods as an episcopalian cathedral. On 23 July 1637, the dean attempted to read the English church service book from the pulpit. Unused to this system of worship, the congregation rioted, and one of the leaders of the commotion was a market stall-holder called Jenny Geddes. At a time when it was normal practice for church congregations to bring their own seats to church, Jenny Geddes is said to have thrown her stool at the dean, shouting 'Dost thou say mass at ma lug?' A tablet at the entrance to the Moray Aisle commemorates the episode.

Flanking St Giles' to the north were *luckenbooths* (or locked booths) on the ground level of the high tenements (blocks of flats). The luckenbooths housed the merchants of the day, right up to the end of the 18th century – shoemakers, snuff-makers, grocers, bakers, drapers, milliners, watchmakers and jewellers.

One such booth was the workshop of George Heriot, goldsmith to King James VI. The name luckenbooth has lived on in the jewellery design representing two entwined hearts, often given as an engagement gift.

Around the buttresses of St Giles' were tiny stalls known as *krames*. These were often open market stalls which specialised in hardware, leather goods and children's toys. Lord Cockburn, a famous 19th-century judge, recalled, 'It was like one of the Arabian Nights bazaars in Bagdad. Let anyone fancy what it was about New Year when every child got its handsel and every farthing of every handsel was spent there. The krames was the paradise of childhood.'

For centuries this was the busiest part of the High Street – a world apart from our present-day shopping malls like Waverley Market, where we do not have to face a biting east wind buffeting the little stalls!

Gladstone's Land

This museum is an interesting reconstruction, by the National Trust for Scotland, of the pattern of 17th-century domestic life in the Royal Mile. In those days, Edinburgh was becoming a very cramped metropolis within its town walls. There was really only one way for the buildings to go – up – and this explains the distinctive and democratic arrangement of the Edinburgh tenements. Lords and lawyers, beggars and blacksmiths often lived on the same stair. It was not till the 18th-century extension of the New Town that the different classes of society began to occupy different areas of the city.

Gladstone's Land is a typical Old Town tenement, dating from about 1550. Thomas Gledstanes and his wife Bessie Cunningham bought the timber-fronted property in 1617. Gledstanes was a merchant and in the 1622 Customs Book for Leith he is shown as trading in prunes, iron, pots, honey and vinegar. He soon set about improving the building (he gave it its stone front) and extending it (forward 7 m into the Lawnmarket as most of his neighbours seem to have been doing at the time, and up to its present six-storey height). Access to all but the ground floors and basement was by an outside stair, or forestair, from the pavement. There is a similar forestair at Moubray House, next to John Knox House.

The two-arch arcade of the ground floor was almost certainly two shop fronts, and is now laid out as a cloth merchant's booth. The cloths displayed are based on materials used in the 17th century. Upstairs the key remains of the period are the original 17th-century painted ceilings.

Records of the period show that the other occupants of the tenement at the time of Thomas Gledstanes were Mr William Strutheris, a minister; Mr John Riddoch, a merchant (like Gledstanes); Sir James Creichton, Kt., a gentleman whose occupation is not recorded; and Mr James Nicolsone, a guild officer who occupied 'the lowest back dwelling house'. There are no details of their families, but one can imagine the everyday lack of privacy within the confines of this narrow building. The occupants even had to sidestep a grunting pig who lived under the forestair!

A visit to Gladstone's Land today gives an excellent insight into 17th-century Edinburgh life. There is an information room and an education room for school parties, with costumes to wear. Try reading *An Edinburgh Reel* by Iona McGregor. Gladstone's Land is the location of this romantic adventure set in 18th-century Edinburgh.

The hanging sign outside the building has a *gled* on top – a Scots word for hawk. A *gled* is also painted on the ceiling of the third floor where Thomas and Bessie Gledstanes lived.

The window shutters on the first two floors were a common feature – glass was still an expensive item, so only the upper half of each window was glazed.

Out of the open shutters the Gledstanes and their tenants would have looked out on the busy Lawnmarket with its stalls, much squalor and poverty, and occasional criminals being led down to the place of execution in the Grassmarket. In the plague years like 1645, bodies of victims would have been carried out from houses, with some families being removed outside the city to the Burgh Muir, until the infection had passed.

In contrast, such stately occasions as the procession of Charles I and his retinue en route to his Scottish coronation at Holyrood Abbey in 1633, would also be viewed through the open shutters.

Gladstone's Land.

Growth of the city: an artist's impression of Edinburgh in about 1250. The original fort on the rock has now become a royal castle with Queen Margaret's Chapel inside it. At the bottom of the Royal Mile, Margaret's son, King David, built the first Holyrood Abbey. There is a wooden town wall and St Giles Kirk has been built. The Burgh Loch (now the Meadows) is on the left.

SALISBURY CRAGS

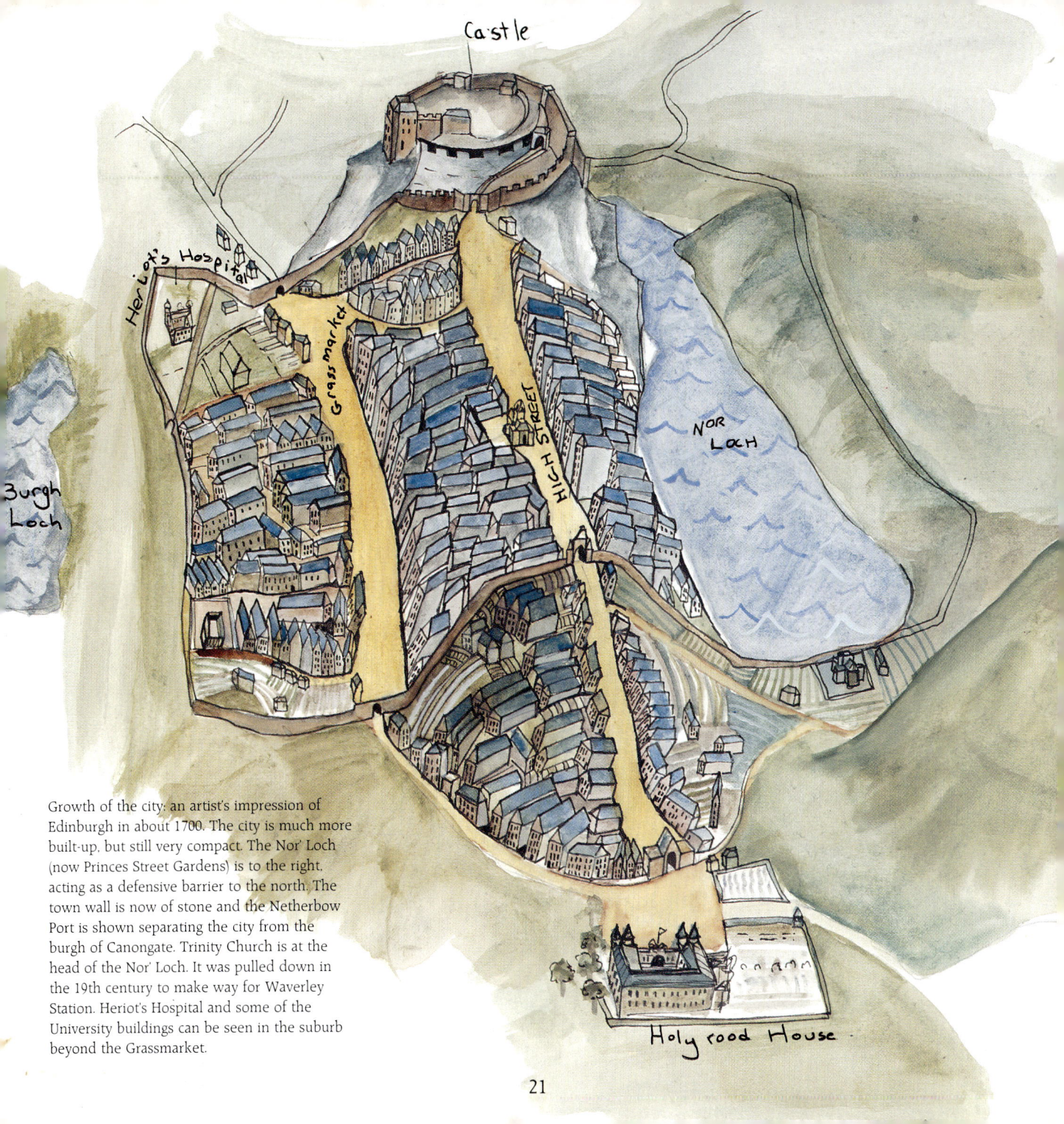

Growth of the city: an artist's impression of Edinburgh in about 1700. The city is much more built-up, but still very compact. The Nor' Loch (now Princes Street Gardens) is to the right, acting as a defensive barrier to the north. The town wall is now of stone and the Netherbow Port is shown separating the city from the burgh of Canongate. Trinity Church is at the head of the Nor' Loch. It was pulled down in the 19th century to make way for Waverley Station. Heriot's Hospital and some of the University buildings can be seen in the suburb beyond the Grassmarket.

Edinburgh's Other Castles

Beyond Edinburgh Castle itself, the city has other castles worth seeking out. MERCHISTON CASTLE was the birthplace of the brilliant mathematician John Napier (see page 41). It has now been cleverly incorporated into the buildings of Napier Polytechnic. Mary Queen of Scots is said to have planted a pear tree in the garden. COLINTON CASTLE is now an ivy-covered ruin – thanks to the attentions of Cromwell! It stands in the grounds of Merchiston Castle School. CRAIGCROOK CASTLE at Blackhall was built in 1545 and was a keep of gun loops and cannon-spouts for the defence of Edinburgh in time of siege. Two castles open to the public are CRAIGMILLAR and LAURISTON.

Craigmillar Castle This is one of Edinburgh's 'other' castles, to the south-east of the city, but within its boundaries since 1920. Craigmillar is only about 4 km from the Old Town of Edinburgh, whose roofs and spires are clearly visible from Craigmillar's tower. It was a favourite retreat for the Stewart kings and queens, especially when life at Holyrood got too turbulent, and it is connected with several key episodes in Scottish history.

The original fortified tower-house of Craigmillar was built in the late 14th/early 15th century by the Preston family, who acquired the barony of Craigmillar in 1374. In style and date it closely resembles the great tower (David's Tower, 1362) of Edinburgh Castle, and may well have used the same builders and architects.

Craigmillar Castle — still a striking local landmark.

Later additions were the courtyard buildings and the Great Chamber, built after the 1544 sacking of the castle and its later reconstruction. There was also a small 15th-century chapel with crow-stepped gables.

All the later additions are located snugly within the castle's inner curtain wall – still almost complete. These massive rectangular defences were added in 1427. The curtain walls are 1.5m thick and 8.5m high, and there are stout round towers at all four corners. A set of outer walls, incorporating an outer courtyard, was added in the 16th century. Even today the well-defended access to the main buildings is most impressive.

Craigmillar had close links with Mary Queen of Scots and James VI. Mary withdrew here for a time in 1566 after the murder of Rizzio at Holyrood. Here too was signed the unholy pact (with or without the Queen's knowledge) to murder Lord Darnley, Mary's husband. And here James VI formed the adventurous plan – for those days – to travel to Norway in person in order to bring home his bride-to-be, Anne of Denmark.

For a ruin, Craigmillar is very complete. So a visit here makes it easy to understand the arrangement and layout of a large baronial residence in the later Middle Ages.

Lauriston Castle, to the north of the city, is now more a mansion than a real castle. But like Craigmillar, it was also developed from an original tower house, built in 1590. It has one of the few remaining historic gardens in the city – a fine example of a 19th-century garden, with a wonderful view over the Forth. (See page 37.)

The main entrance of the curtain wall. Above the gate are the arms of the Preston family who built the castle. Overhead, on the battlements, is the lion rampant of Scotland, which the lord of Craigmillar was entitled to place above his own.

Lauriston Castle showing the old tower house to the left.

The New Town

The New Town of Edinburgh was begun in 1767 and was built up, from east to west, by 1800. The plan was the work of a young architect called James Craig, and it won a competition organised by the City Fathers. As we have seen, the Old Town was by this time bursting at the seams, its streets unhygienic and many of its buildings in danger of collapse.

James Craig's plan was for a layout of spacious parallel streets – or 'windy parallelograms' – with spectacular open views south from Princes Street and north from Queen Street. Two fine squares were planned to contain the east and west end of the development. In order to link Old and New Towns, the Nor' Loch had been drained after 1759, and the building of the North Bridge was undertaken (opened to traffic in 1772). Later the Mound was built, using stones and earth from the New Town excavations where nearly all the houses had cellars.

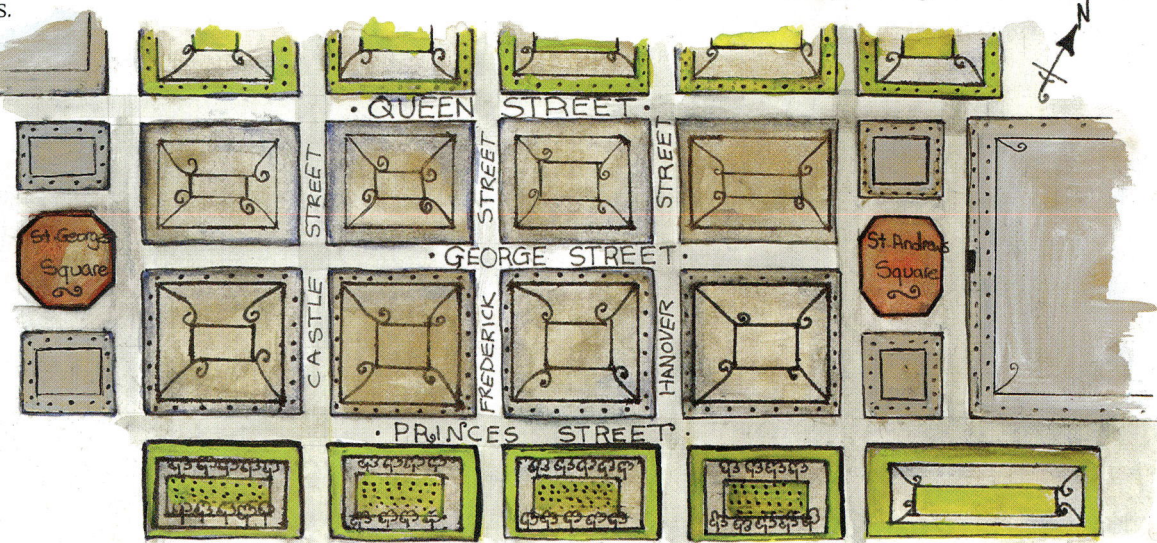

James Craig: a portrait by David Allan in the National Portrait Gallery, Edinburgh.

'Plan of the new streets and squares intended for the City of Edinburgh, 1767' by James Craig.

Walking across Princes Street Gardens today, it is hard to imagine what an effective barrier this once wet and marshy area was. There is a story that David Hume, the 18th-century thinker and philosopher, slipped on a footpath through the marsh one day on an outing to see how work on his New Town house was progressing. A passing Newhaven fishwife set down her wares and made to help him regain the safety of the path, for he was in danger of sinking into the bog. Recognising the famous man, she drew back and told him it might not be proper for a Christian woman like herself to help a notorious unbeliever like Hume. She eventually agreed to help him if he would first say the Lord's Prayer with her. She was surprised to discover that he knew the prayer off by heart, and she duly helped him back to safe ground.

David Hume's new house was in St David's Street. The street got its name as a joke played on its famous inhabitant. Most of the other streets are named after members of the royal family at the time.

In addition to splendid housing and wide vistas, many fine public buildings were erected - the Assembly Rooms, Register House, the National Gallery and the Royal Scottish Academy. There were also several fine churches - St Andrew's, St Cuthbert's, St John's, St George's (now West Register House) - and numerous statues and monuments. The Scott Monument is the most spectacular, but look also for the tall Melville Monument (41 m, to Henry Dundas, Lord Melville, the powerful late 18th-century politician) in St Andrew Square surveying the length of George Street. The fine statues of King George IV and prime minister William Pitt are now in use as latter-day traffic roundabouts in George Street. Wellington on his charger is in front of Register House (does it rear up in fright at the noise of the traffic?) - while Prince Albert sits astride a more sedate beast among the trees in Charlotte Square.

Before long, the New Town was a great success, and many leading Edinburgh citizens moved here as soon as houses became available. This success led to the development of the Northern New Town from 1802, and the Western New Town and the Moray Estates a few years later.

The National Gallery of Scotland and the Royal Scottish Academy designed by William Playfair to look like Greek temples. These buildings - and the National Monument - gave Edinburgh the name 'Athens of the north'.

The Georgian House

It is not easy to appreciate the nature or the variety of the domestic improvements which were coming about at the time of the building of the New Town. At last houses were being built with large airy rooms and lots of windows, and an age of elegance was arriving. But there were as yet few plumbed-in lavatories - piped water supplies were still in their infancy and most houses in the New Town relied on a pump in the scullery which drew water from a well at the back of the house. Drains and sewage discharged into a cesspool which was emptied at night into a cart by the night soil men.

The best way to appreciate the spacious living arrangements of the New Town in the late 18th century is to visit the Georgian House at 7 Charlotte Square. This property belongs to the National Trust for Scotland, and the rooms are furnished and decorated as they might have been at the time of the first owners.

Just as Gladstone's Land (see page 18) is a typical example of a 17th-century dwelling in the Old Town, so the Georgian House is a typical example of a late 18th-century New Town dwelling.

The north side of Charlotte Square - of which No 7 is part - was designed by Robert Adam and built in the 1790s. The style is influenced by Roman architecture, with its columns, roof ornaments and symmetrical arrangements. Notice the raised pavements on the street, with mounting blocks for easy access to carriages.

The Georgian House.

Inside, everything has been arranged to give the visitor a picture of the period and the way of life. The furniture and fittings, the paintings and ornaments, the interior decoration, fabrics, curtains and coverings have all been chosen with this aim. There is a formal drawing room stretching the full width of the house; a ground floor dining room arranged for a formal dinner party with Wedgwood china and Sheffield plate; and next-door a bedchamber with superb four-poster bed.

The kitchen, in the basement, has a splendid range – the roasting spit is linked by a system of gears and pulleys to a fan in the chimney. The greater the heat from the fire, the faster the fan turned and the faster the spit revolved. Cooking was still laborious – the iron or copper pots, scoured out with sand, were very heavy. Although large establishments had ice houses in the grounds, most people living in the New Town relied on cool cellars and larders to keep food as fresh as possible. Meat and fish were preserved with salt, hams were smoked, vegetables were dried and pickled and fruit dried and bottled. Fresh foods were bought from the markets in the Old Town – fruit and vegetables from market gardens around the city; poultry including wild duck and goose, and gannet from the Bass Rock; trout from Loch Leven and shellfish from Musselburgh; meat and fish would have been bought in Fleshmarket and Fishmarket Closes.

In the late 1700s/early 1800s there was still no gas or electricity. Candles and rush-lights were the only form of lighting. Coal had to be heaved around the house for fires. You can imagine the army of servants which looked after the day-to-day arrangements of this elegant town house.

The interior elegance of a New Town house.

The port of Leith.

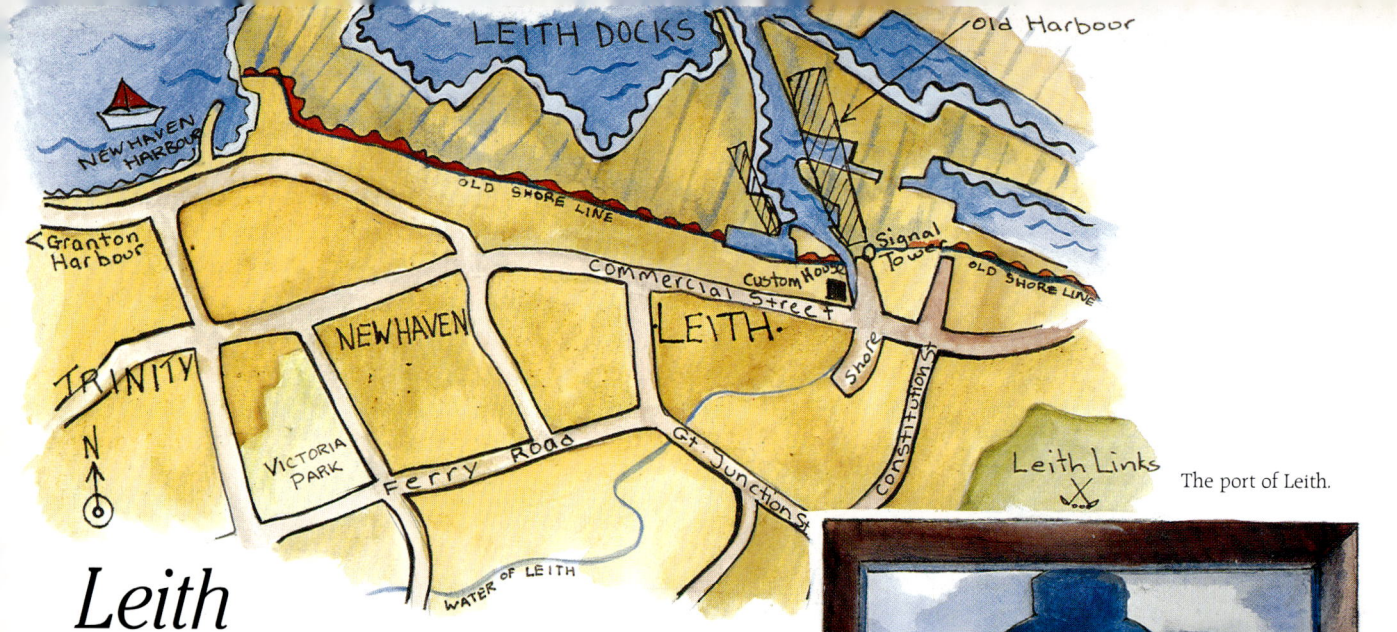

Leith

The chief port of Scotland by about 1450, Leith traded with England, the Baltic, the Low Countries and France. The wine trade with Bordeaux, and the export of salt fish and hides date from very early days. The vaults in Giles Street have stored wine since the 15th century. Leith also had a fishing trade in herring and oysters by this date, and shipbuilding was a third mainstay of Leith's economy right up to the present century.

By the 18th century, coastal fishing was giving way to whaling and deep-sea fishing. There was a ferry between Leith and Kinghorn in Fife, and the Leith smacks were in fierce competition with the stagecoaches and the turnpike roads to convey travellers to and from London.

Today the port area has deepwater facilities and has been greatly increased in area by land reclamation. As a result, the sea is nowhere really visible in Leith today. Names like Custom House, The Shore, Signal Tower and Dock Place look rather landlocked, beached like the whales that used to be brought here in Christian Salvesen's factory ships. (Edinburgh Zoo's fine penguin collection is a result of Leith's Antarctic whaling connections.)

Leith Links - still open parkland - was probably the home of golf, being at least 13 years older than St Andrews. John Knox and King Charles I are both reputed to have swung their clubs here.

King's Landing today. George IV landed here with great pomp and ceremony on his visit to Edinburgh in 1822. It was the first visit of a British monarch to Scotland for nearly 200 years. Sir Walter Scott devised and 'stage-managed' the celebrations.

Street names are another reminder of the town's maritime connections – Baltic, Coburg, Elbe and Cadiz. A good map of the world shows another Leith Harbour – in South Georgia, where the whaling fleet used to moor.

The Boundary Bar, halfway up Leith Walk, still marks the old municipal boundary between Leith and Edinburgh before their amalgamation in 1920. This is a reminder of the fact that in the 19th century Leith was a separate and flourishing burgh, with its own town hall, burgh court and police force. (A joke from this time was to try to say quickly, 'The Leith police dismisseth us.') However, there is still a small link with the Old Town of Edinburgh – a sludge boat named *Gardyloo* plies out from Leith to beyond the Isle of May in the Forth.

Leith today is being transformed. Its handsome public buildings are being restored – the Corn Exchange, Customs House, Leith Assembly Rooms, Old Leith Bank. Its river – the Water of Leith – has been cleaned up, Leith Walk is now treelined and looks like a Parisian boulevard, old warehouses have been converted into attractive blocks of flats, and there is a growing range of smart restaurants where once there were only seamen's pubs.

Water of Leith Edinburgh's river, the Water of Leith, rises in the moorland of the Pentland Hills and was a vital source of power and water for the many mills along its length. Paper, snuff, flour and timber mills, bleach works, dye works and tanneries all depended on this small river.

As these industries declined, or sought another source of power, the river and the land surrounding it became run-down and neglected. In the 1970s a lengthy clean-up operation began and long stretches of the Water of Leith Walkway have been built from the outskirts of the city to Leith. Via this wonderfully varied corridor of wildlife and industrial archaeology, you are now able to walk from: Balerno - Juniper Green - Slateford; Roseburn - Stockbridge - Deanhaugh; Warriston - Coburg Street; Sandport Place, Leith. En route you can see nearly 150 different plant species, as well as a variety of birds and evidence of roe deer and badgers. The Water of Leith is also stocked annually with trout.

Villages of Edinburgh

The city of Edinburgh covers a wide area today, but only in the last 100 years has it swallowed up entire surrounding communities. You can read about Leith and Craigmillar on pages 28 and 22. The following is a selection of some of the oldest villages within the city - Corstorphine, Cramond, Dean and Duddingston.

Corstorphine There is an old parish church here, dating from about 1400. The grey stone-slabbed roof is very solid-looking, and on the east end of the church is a lamp niche. This was a beacon - a sort of lighthouse - which guided travellers from Edinburgh past the large marshy area east of the church. The beacon was in regular use from 1429 until 1769.

Inside the building are fine old tombs with effigies of the local Forrester family, the oldest dating to 1405.

Cramond This is a favourite beauty spot for walks. Cramond Glebe Road with its whitewashed inn and cottages is picturesque and well-restored, and there are remains of a Roman fort, a 17th-century church (with 19th-century 'improvements'), and a medieval tower house.

The village is at the mouth of the River Almond where it enters the Forth, a safe mooring for Roman warships, and still popular as a sailing anchorage today. A favourite walk is along the east side of the Almond about a mile upstream to Cramond Brig (built about 1500). It was here, according to a popular story, that King James V was rescued from attack by a local tenant farmer called Jock Howison. You pass en route the remains of several mills and weirs - Cockle Mill, Fairafar Mill, Peggy's Mill and Dowie's Mill. They were iron, grain, paper and sawmills in their day.

Another favourite outing from Cramond is across in the little ferry to the Dalmeny estate. You can then walk along the foreshore to South Queensferry past Dalmeny House and Barnbougle Castle.

Duddingston Set between its loch and marshes on the one hand and the lower slopes of Arthur's Seat on the other, Duddingston village has a delightful location. The Norman kirk dates from the 12th-century and contains memorials of the Preston family of nearby Craigmillar Castle (see page 22).

Duddingston Kirk.

The Baxters' symbols are still visible on the old granary building in the Dean Village. The lettering reads, 'In the sweat of thy face, shall thou eat bread.' Gen. 3 Verse 19 ANNO DOM 1619

At the entrance to the kirkyard is an octagonal watchtower (1824), built to prevent the practice of bodysnatching. Nearby is a 17th-century loupin-on stane (a platform for the less athletic members of the congregation to mount and dismount their horses), and a jougs-collar, a device for punishing villagers who had committed sins.

Between the kirkyard and the loch is Dr Neil's Garden, derelict ground until 1967, but now a charming lochside garden. Thomson's Tower is the name of the octagonal curling house (1823, by Playfair) at the east end of the garden. It reminds visitors of the local importance of curling – the Duddingston Curling Society is one of the oldest in Scotland. The loch is also a popular bird sanctuary for geese and ducks.

Dean The Dean Village is now a peaceful and picturesque residential backwater, only ten minutes' walk from the west end of Princes Street. Dean's beginnings were in the 12th century when numerous mills were built to supply meal to the surrounding communities. The mills were run by the Incorporation of Baxters (or bakers), and several buildings in the village have memorials in stone to the old millers and their work.

Duddingston Watchtower.

The Hills of Edinburgh

Like Athens, Rome, San Francisco and Rio de Janeiro, and a few other lucky places, Edinburgh is blessed with a splendid natural setting. It is not flat and uninteresting. It comes at you from all angles and levels. If you walk across the Meadows, or up Easter Road, or east down Regent Road, you cannot but be struck by the mass of Arthur's Seat and the Salisbury Crags. Princes Street and the Gardens are dominated by the Castle Rock, as is the drive into the city along the Western Approach Road.

Arthur's Seat and the Castle Rock are only two of Edinburgh's hills. Others are Calton Hill, Blackford Hill, Braid Hill, Craiglockhart Hill and Corstorphine Hill. And just as the hills of Edinburgh look striking and dramatic from street level below, so too the view from the top of some of the hills can be impressive and surprising. Sunsets can be very special, with the turrets, towers and spires of the city silhouetted like purple velvet against a flaming sky.

Arthur's Seat is the main feature of Holyrood Park. Edinburgh's highest hill (251m), an extinct volcanic plug, it can be approached from several starting points. The easiest way is to drive up the Queen's Drive (which circles the park) to Dunsapie Loch, where there is a car park (113m) and walk the rest of the way. Unless the weather is poor, you will probably have company of all ages, shapes and sizes, for this is a popular outing. On 1 May, Arthur's Seat can be positively busy with summer-worshippers out to see the sun rise. There is a direction finder on the summit. Strong shoes are recommended for this walk, which involves some rock scrambling near the summit.

A longer approach is from Holyroodhouse, via a tarred footpath past St Margaret's Well. This brings you up to the Hunter's Bog, where archers used to do target practice, and by keeping this flat valley to the right you climb the main bulk of the hill.

A third walk, which affords the best views of the town, follows the Radical Road under the Salisbury Crags. The Radical Road was constructed in 1820, on the advice of Sir Walter Scott, by unemployed workmen who were beginning to agitate for work, egged on by Radical politicians (the Labour party of the period).

The panorama of Holyrood Park, dominated by Arthur's Seat.

Edinburgh's hills.

Calton Hill is visible due east of Princes Street, with a cluster of interesting buildings at its summit (100m). Access is easy and not too strenuous. There are steps for pedestrians from Regent Road, and a road for vehicles behind the Crown Office Buildings. The panoramas of the city from Calton Hill are probably the finest of all – across to the North Bridge and the Castle, Princes Street and the spires of the New Town, north to the Forth and the Fife hills.

The buildings on Calton Hill are the Old City Observatory, the National Monument *à la* Parthenon ('Scotland's disgrace') and the Nelson Tower, which can be climbed.

If you climb Calton Hill around 1 pm, you can watch out of one eye for the puff of smoke from the Castle ramparts swiftly followed by the noise of the 1 o'clock gun. With your other eye, if you are quick, watch out for the almost simultaneous dropping of the time-ball, the large black cylinder affixed to the white mast on top of the Nelson Tower. This daily event dates to the period when ships on the Forth set their timepieces by the dropping of the time-ball, observed through the ships' telescopes. The monument itself was designed in the shape of an upturned telescope.

Nelson Tower on Calton Hill.

Salisbury Crags Radical Road Queen's Drive

Parks, Gardens and Animal Magic

A city that is built on seven hills is likely to be fortunate in its open spaces. And so it proves.

Princes Street Gardens. Bounded on one side by the length of Princes Street and on the other by the Castle Rock, these are well laid out with flowerbeds, fine vistas and seats. Popular with visitors and locals alike, especially in summer when there may be music from the Ross Bandstand or more spontaneous informal entertainment during the Festival months of August and September.

The gardens are laid out on the bed of the old Nor' Loch, drained in the 18th century in preparation for the development of the New Town. They are divided by the Mound into East and West Gardens. The East Gardens contain the Scott Monument (see page 38) and good views of the trains at Waverley Station.

Worth a visit in the West Gardens, especially on the hour if you want to see the cuckoo in action, is the Floral Clock, which is the oldest in the world and has entertained visitors since 1904. Each year the clock is planted out with up to 24,000 dwarf plants (lobelias, pyrethrums, echeveria, sedums, etc.). There is a fountain and toddlers' play area at the west end of the park. There are many statues and monuments, but of especial interest is the 9 m long Scottish/American memorial to soldiers of World War I, and the relief carving below the Floral Clock dedicated to The Royal Scots.

Edinburgh Zoo is on Corstorphine Road to the west of the city and extends up the slope of Corstorphine Hill. It is a comprehensive collection, financed by admission fees and subscriptions. A popular daily event in the summer months is the penguin parade. At 14.30 hours there is a (voluntary!) penguin parade as the birds follow one of the keepers round the open space outside the penguin enclosure before they all return to captivity to be fed. There is a visitors' picnic area, a restaurant, and an education centre for local schoolchildren. Many schools and other organisations 'sponsor' an animal.

Floral Clock.

Penguin parade.

Gorgie City Farm, formerly old railway sidings and still bounded by tenements, has a whole host of animals and birds on display. It is a community farm - almost in the city centre - and actively encourages children to join in the farm work.

Water of Leith Walkway (see also page 28). The Walkway beside the Water of Leith has been developed since the 1970s. The suburban section from Balerno to Slateford is 8 km and mostly follows the track of a disused railway. There is a tunnel section at Colinton Dell, and several disused mills.

The town section from Roseburn to Canonmills (4.8 km) introduces explorers to such picturesque backwaters as the Dean Village, and takes you past the circular Roman temple of St Bernard's Well (1790), then via Stockbridge and the 'Colonies' – 2 storey terraces of flatted cottages laid out in 1861 by the Edinburgh Cooperative Building Association.

St Bernard's Well.

Saughton Park contains one of the best play areas (Fort Saughton) in the city, with swings, climbing frames, seesaws, etc. There is also a fine formal rose-garden (with braille nametags for the blind), an enclosed plant-house, and good summer floral displays.

Hermitage of Braid/Blackford Hill. The 18th-century House of the Hermitage is now a countryside information centre. The Hermitage estate lies in the deep, tree-covered valley of the Braid Burn and is a perfect example of 'the country in the town'. At its eastern end, there is access to the Blackford Hill, with its Observatory and Blackford Pond. The hilltop (164m) has a viewfinder and fine vistas north over the city. If you continue east down the Braid Burn keeping Blackford Hill to your left, you come to an old quarry. The rock face is nowadays popular with rockclimbers and scramblers. Here too, in the mid 19th century, the Swiss geologist Louis Agassiz decided that some of the grooves in the rockface were caused by glaciation – a novel idea in those days.

The Royal Botanic Garden is among the finest in Britain, and was laid out in 1820-23. Features include the Rock Garden, with its wonderful alpines; the Arboretum, with trees from all over the world; the plant houses, where plants from tropical, desert and other climates are displayed; the demonstration garden; the rhododendron walks; and the magnificent herbaceous border beneath its splendid beech hedge.

The Aboretum at the Royal Botanic Garden.

Museums, Galleries and Other Interesting Places to Visit

IN AND AROUND THE ROYAL MILE

The People's Story,   Canongate Tolbooth, Canongate
Formerly a courthouse and prison, this 16th-century building is now a museum and tells of the lives, work and pastimes of the ordinary men and women of Edinburgh from the 18th century to the present day. Reconstructions of the work of a town crier, cooper, fishwife and clippie on a tram are imaginatively presented in sight and sound. Well worth a visit. (Free. Mon.–Sat. 10.00–17.00.)

Huntly House Museum,   142 Canongate
Almost opposite the Canongate Tolbooth, this was formerly known as 'The Speaking House' because of the Latin mottoes on its walls. Now a Municipal Museum, it has fascinating displays of material from the city's history and public life. (Free. Mon.-Sat. 10.00-17.00.)

John Knox House,   45 High Street
Many relics of the famous reformer and of the Reformation. The house is 15th century, with good views up the High Street towards St Giles. Old Town enquiry/information centre, linked with nextdoor Netherbow Arts Centre. (Admission charge. Mon.-Sat. 10.00-17.00.)

John Knox House.

Canongate Church.

Canongate Churchyard,   Canongate Church
The churchyard contains graves of many famous Scots - the poet Robert Fergusson, the lord provost George Drummond whose foresight developed the New Town of Edinburgh, Adam Smith, the economist - study the details on the tombstones.

Below Canongate Church is Dunbar's Close Garden - a reconstruction of a 17th-century garden. These Old Town gardens were a useful source of medicinal plants.

Brass Rubbing Centre, Trinity Apse,   Chalmers Close (off High Street)
A fascinating collection of replicas moulded from ancient Pictish stones, rare Scottish brasses and medieval church brasses. No experience needed - materials are provided. (Free. Mon.-Sat. 10.00-17.00.)

Museum of Childhood,   38 High Street
The history of children's toys and amusements - the first of its kind. A storehouse of nostalgia for mums and dads, a treasure chest of delights for children. (Free. Mon.-Sat. 10.00-18.00.)

Lady Stair's House,   Lawnmarket
A 17th-century town house with interesting artefacts from the lives of three great Scottish men of letters: Robert Burns, Sir Walter Scott and Robert Louis Stevenson. (Free. Mon.-Fri. 10.00-17.00.)

Gladstone's Land,   Lawnmarket
See page 18. (Admission charge. Mon.-Sat. 10.00-17.00. Sun. 14.00-17.00.)

Camera Obscura and the **Outlook Tower,**   Castlehill (See page 11.)
On a clear day, a wonderful vantage point to view the city. (Admission charge. Open daily.)

IN AND AROUND THE NEW TOWN

National Gallery of Scotland,   2 The Mound
Fine collection of European and British painting. Scottish artists including Allan Ramsay and Sir Henry Raeburn are well represented. Look for Raeburn's most famous portrait of Sir Walter Scott - the two gifted men were friends. (Free. Mon.-Sat. 10.00-17.00. Sun. 14.00-17.00.)

Royal Scottish Academy,   1 The Mound
The seated statue of Queen Victoria (representing Britannia) was added to the front of the building in 1844. Annual exhibitions of Scottish artists' work and other exhibitions. (Admission charge. Mon.-Sat. 10.00-17.00. Sun. 14.00-17.00.)

Royal Museum of Scotland,   2 Queen Street
A rich collection of prehistoric remains, Scottish historical displays and exhibits of medieval life and art. Here you can see John Knox's pulpit and Jenny Geddes' stool (see page 17), the Traprain Treasure and the Lewis chessmen. (Free. Mon.-Sat. 10.00-17.00. Sun. 14.00-17.00.)

Scottish National Portrait Gallery,   2 Queen Street
A display, starting with the Stewart kings, and including many contemporary figures from Scottish politics, business and culture. Also houses the Scottish Photography Archive. (Free. Mon.-Sat. 10.00-18.00. Sun. 11.00-18.00.)

The Georgian House,   7 Charlotte Square (See page 26.)
(Admission charge. Mon.-Sat. 10.00-17.00. Sun. 14.00-17.00. Closed mid-December to April.)

New Town Conservation Centre,   13A Dundas Street
A past, present and future look at the New Town of Edinburgh. (Free. Mon.-Fri. 09.00-13.00; 14.00-17.00.)

Scott Monument,   Princes Street Gardens (See pages 34 and 38.)
A dizzying spiral staircase takes you to the top of this Victorian Gothic landmark. (Admission charge.)

OTHER LOCATIONS

Royal Museum of Scotland,   Chambers Street
The building was opened in 1866 and houses four major departments: (i) History and Applied Art, (ii) Natural History, (iii) Geology, (iv) Science, Technology and Working Life. Some special exhibitions, regular lectures and events. (Free. Mon.-Sat. 10.00-17.00. Sun. 14.00-17.00.)

Royal Observatory.

Royal Observatory,   Blackford Hill
An insight into the work of the observatory at home and abroad. A wide variety of displays and a unique collection of antique telescopes. (Admission charge. Mon.-Fri. 10.00-16.00. Weekends and Holidays 12.00-17.00.)

Lauriston Castle,   Cramond Road South (See page 22.)
A furnished castle/dwelling house which gives a good idea of the affluent lifestyle of the 1890s and early 20th century. Secret passage and hidey hole. Pleasant grounds overlook the Forth. (Admission charge. April to October. Daily, except Fri. 11.00-13.00; 14.00-17.00. Nov.-March Sat. & Sun. only.)

National Gallery of Modern Art,   Belford Road
Formerly John Watson's School, built in Greek Doric style by William Burn, 1825. Most modern masters - Picasso, Hepworth, Matisse and Moore included - are represented, and there is an excellent collection of modern Scottish artists including MacTaggart, Peploe, Hornel, Eardley, Crawhall. Some sculpture in the garden. (Free. Mon.-Sat. 10.00-17.00. Sun. 14.00-17.00.)

Monuments and Statues

Edinburgh is rich in memorials in stone and metal recalling episodes from its history. A few of the most intriguing and famous are listed here.

The Scott Monument   (East Princes Street Gardens)
This memorial to one of Edinburgh's most famous sons was completed in 1846, only 14 years after his death. It is a rather blackened sandstone Gothic steeple rising 61m over a white marble statue of Sir Walter and his dog Maida. There are niche statues of more than 60 of Scott's famous fictional characters. The monument is open to the public and may be climbed - if you have a good head for heights. There are 287 steps, getting narrower and narrower towards the top, but there are good views of Jenner's restaurant (close up), the rooftops of the New Town and further afield.

Greyfriars Bobby Memorial   (Candlemaker Row/George IV Bridge)
This is a small bronze statue of John Gray's faithful terrier dog. After John Gray's death in 1858, Bobby spent his days watching at his master's grave in Greyfriars Cemetery and his nights sheltering under a nearby table gravestone. Bobby's vigil lasted 14 years. His dinner dish, drinking cup and collar, as well as a fuller account of his life, can be seen in Huntly House Museum. (Also try reading *Tale of Greyfriar's Bobby* by Lavinia Derwent, or Eleanor Atkinson's version of the same story for older children.)

Scott Monument.

Greyfriars Bobby.

The Witches' Fountain (Castle Esplanade)
This bronze fountain was built in 1894, to commemorate the 300 witches burnt on Castle Hill between 1492 and 1722. There is a picture of witches' heads entwined by a serpent. The serpent is the symbol of Aesculapius, who was the Greek god of medicine. It reminds us that many so-called witches were active in homeopathic medicine, and did not all work for evil ends.

King Charles II (Parliament Square)
This is an equestrian statue in lead dating from 1685, which makes it the oldest in Edinburgh. It cost the Town Council £2580, which was a lot of money in those days. Originally they planned to put a statue of Cromwell there, but the Restoration of the King forced a change of mind. Periodic repairs are necessary, especially to the horse's legs - which have suffered from metal fatigue over the years.

Mercat Cross (High Street/east of St Giles' High Kirk)
The Mercat, or Market, Cross was a symbol of the burgh's trading rights, and its right to hold markets and fairs. It was also where royal proclamations were read out, and where business was transacted in the 18th century before the Royal Exchange was built across the road in 1754 (now the City Chambers). It was also the site of many public executions, including that of the Marquis of Montrose in 1650.

The original Mercat Cross dated to the 14th century. The present one was erected in 1885 by William Gladstone, the great Victorian prime minister and MP for Midlothian.

National Monument (Calton Hill)
This was to be a copy of the Parthenon in Athens, a memorial to the fallen in the Napoleonic Wars, containing a Hall of Heroes with statues of the great men and women of Scottish history. Building began in 1826, but ran out of funds and was never completed. So the National Monument is better known locally as 'Scotland's disgrace'.

King Charles II.

National Monument, Calton Hill. In a letter written by the architect, William Playfair he said, 'It takes twelve horses and 70 men to move some of the larger stones up the hill.'

Famous People

The rich character of Edinburgh is made up of the cross-section of its citizens. From artists, architects, churchmen, musicians, doctors, lawyers, writers, philosophers, pioneers and explorers, printers and publishers and many others, Edinburgh has great wealth and diversity in its heritage. It owes much to its famous citizens for making the city the memorable place it is today.

John Knox (c 1505-1572). Edinburgh has many associations with the Reformation - that great religious revolution which swept away the old Catholic faith. Knox is remembered today as one of the fathers of the reformed Church of Scotland. In his *Book of Common Discipline*, he described the constitution of a presbyterian church, as well as a national education system from parish school to university, and a programme of poor relief. He was minister of St Giles' Kirk from 1561, and it was from this post that he defended the fledgling Church of Scotland against the Roman Catholic Mary Queen of Scots after her return from France.

Edinburgh has two statues of Knox: one inside St Giles' and the other looking down the Mound from the Assembly Hall. The latter shows him as an Old Testament prophet, arm uplifted and beard flowing in the wind. John Knox House in the High Street is now a museum, and contains many articles connected with his life.

Sir Walter Scott (1771-1832), perhaps Edinburgh's most famous son, was born in College Wynd, and educated at the Royal High School and the University. He became a lawyer and was called to the Scottish bar in 1792. Interested from his youth in the old ballads and stories of the Scottish borders, Scott soon began to write long narrative poems of his own - 'The Lay of the Last

John Knox.

Minstrel', 'The Lady of the Lake', etc. His novels were huge bestsellers in their day, and created throughout Europe a great cult of romantic interest in Scottish culture. Scott was heavily involved in the bankruptcy of his publisher, James Ballantyne, and it was partly in order to pay off Ballantyne's debts that Scott set himself a very heavy work programme, writing steadily and long into the night. Scott's best novels are probably the Scottish historical ones, such as *Rob Roy*, *Heart of Midlothian*, *Redgauntlet* and *Old Mortality*.

Robert Louis Stevenson (1850-1894) was one of Edinburgh's most famous men of letters. Like Scott, he qualified as a lawyer after Edinburgh University, but turned to writing for a livelihood. Stevenson suffered from a serious chest complaint, and his poor health drove him to live in kinder climates than Edinburgh offers. He travelled widely in Europe, North America and the South Seas, and spent his last years in Samoa. Stevenson's best-known poetry is published in *A Child's Garden of Verses*, which contains many recollections of his childhood, including the well-loved 'Leerie the Lamplighter'.

His famous novels include *Treasure Island*, *Kidnapped* and its sequel *Catriona*, *Dr Jekyll and Mr Hyde*, and *The Master of Ballantrae*.

Robert Louis Stevenson.

David Hume.

David Hume (1711-1776) and **Adam Smith** (1723-1790) were two brilliant and internationally famous thinkers, or philosophers, of 18th century Edinburgh. Hume's most famous book was the *Treatise of Human Nature*, which tried to introduce a sceptical and experimental method of reasoning into moral subjects. Hume was a sceptic in outlook, and an atheist, which was unusual in those days, and made it rather difficult for him to get a job.

Hume's younger friend Adam Smith was one of the fathers of economics, and his most famous book was *Wealth of Nations*, which examined the basic ideas of free markets - division of labour, the function of the marketplace, mediums of exchange and international implications. He attacked tariff barriers and the European theories of wealth based on land.

James Young Simpson (1811-1870) was a doctor and, from the young age of 28, Professor of Midwifery at the University of Edinburgh. He challenged the medieval practices which still attended childbirth, and in 1847 he discovered the anaesthetic properties of chloroform in childbirth. He founded gynaecology, the branch of medicine which specialises in women's diseases, and became physician to Queen Victoria in Scotland.

John Napier (1550-1617) was a famous mathematician who invented logarithms, and a calculating apparatus called Napier's bones, an invention for multiplying and dividing by means of rods - the earliest form of calculating machine.

Deacon Brodie based on a drawing by John Kay.

Edinburgh Baddies

You can imagine that some dark and wicked deeds have been committed in Edinburgh down the years. Here are the stories of three wicked Williams.

William Brodie   In 1788, William Brodie was a deacon (president of his trade), and town councillor of Edinburgh. Councillors were prosperous and respectable citizens, leaders of the community whose affairs they looked after. Deacon Brodie was a prosperous master-carpenter, well-known throughout the town, living in Brodie's Court off the Lawnmarket – maybe a bit of a dandy, with his silver buckled shoes and fine lace collar. At night, people sometimes reported seeing him in the pubs drinking and gambling in the company of rogues. In fact, there was much more to Deacon Brodie than his respectable daytime appearance suggested.

Over the previous two years, several very daring robberies had been carried out in Edinburgh. They were always carried out at night. Money and precious articles were stolen, and the thieves never left any damage behind them. Locked doors seemed to be no hindrance to them – they seemed able to pass through them without difficulty.

Eventually a member of the gang of thieves confessed to the police that they had duplicate keys to fit the locks of the doors of all the places that had been robbed. And who had supplied all the doors and locks? Yes – it was the Deacon. Brodie fled from Edinburgh before he could be arrested, but was eventually captured in Amsterdam and shipped home for trial. He was found guilty and hanged outside the Tolbooth jail, the first town councillor who was also a house-breaker and thief.

The true story of Deacon Brodie was the inspiration behind the famous fictional story of *Dr Jekyll and Mr Hyde*, by Robert Louis Stevenson.

William Burke and William Hare This is also a true story, and something of a horror story as well. In the 1820s Edinburgh University's medical school was already famous and students came from far and near to study the anatomy of the human body.

Burke and Hare were labourers in Edinburgh. They discovered that the medical school could never get enough dead bodies to use for their lectures in anatomy. They also found that they could earn £10 by providing fresh bodies in good condition.

Usually bodies were supplied to the medical school by the 'resurrectionists', or body snatchers, groups of scoundrels who went around the city's graveyards digging up recently buried corpses which they then sold to the medical school. This was bad enough, but Burke and Hare went a step further. They started to kill old men and women residents of the lodging house where Burke was working as manager. They would give their victims too much to drink, smother them, and then under cover of darkness deliver their corpses to the medical school. At least sixteen bodies were disposed of in this gruesome way.

Eventually they were discovered and arrested, and Burke was hanged in 1829. Hare escaped from custody, and was never seen again.

The old Edinburgh Tolbooth beside St Giles. Deacon Brodie spent his last night here.

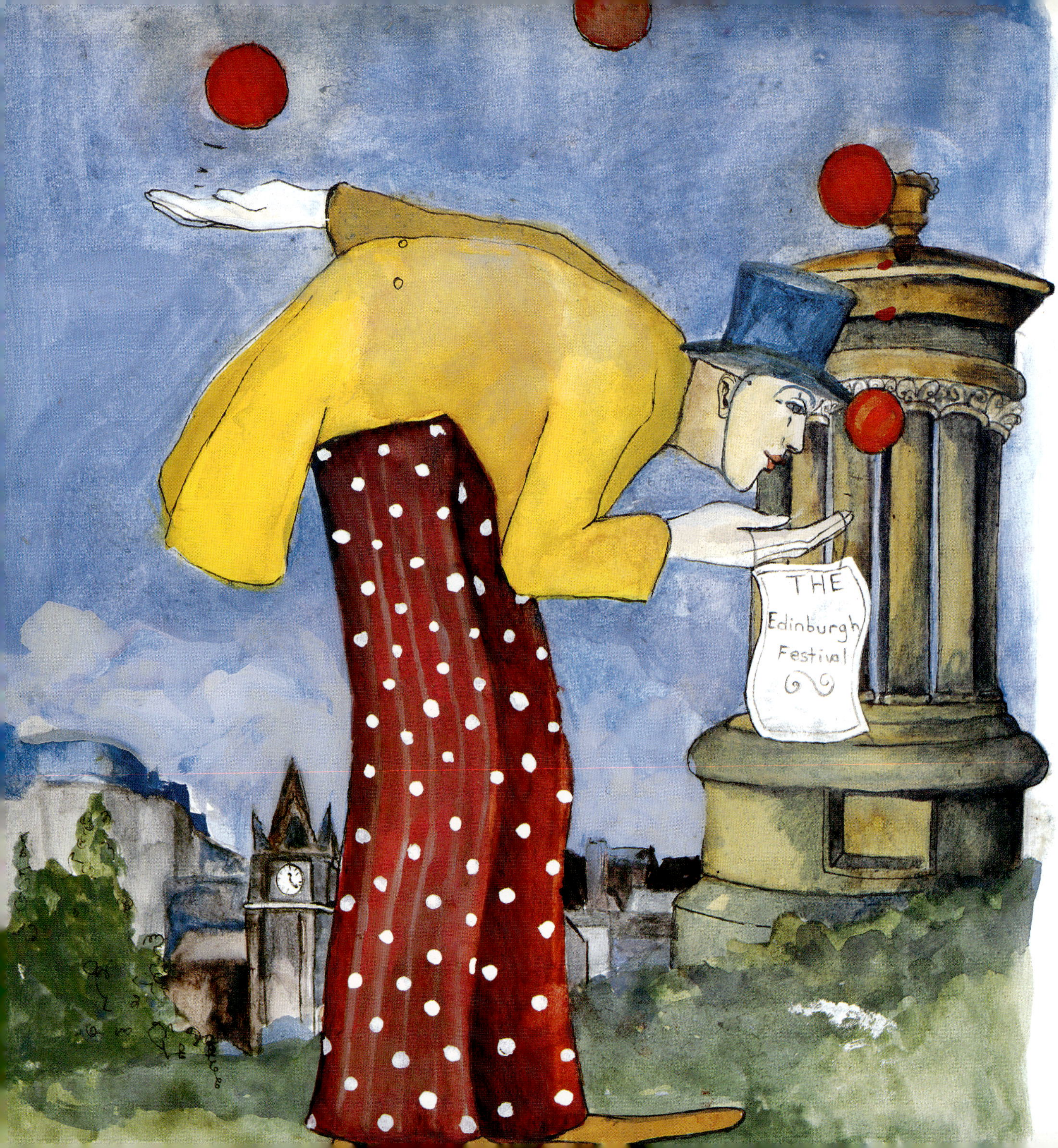
THE
Edinburgh
Festival

The Edinburgh International Festival

There is one period in the year when Edinburgh bursts with life, and bustle, and cultural activity: that is the three-week period at the end of August and beginning of September which is the duration of the Edinburgh International Festival.

During this festive period, visitors flock to the city from every part of the world. The streets take on a carnival atmosphere, and street entertainments flourish for a brief season. The 'Official' Festival has successfully offered a feast of first-rank music and drama since its beginnings in 1947. Around this official core of events, the Festival Fringe has grown from spontaneous beginnings in 1947 with 8 visiting companies to a programme almost bewildering in its variety of over 500 plays, concerts, children's events, exhibitions, circuses, etc. Official events are staged in principal venues such as the Usher Hall, King's Theatre, Queen's Hall and Playhouse Theatre, while the Fringe occupies whatever accommodation it can find – church halls, leisure centres, schools, pubs, student unions, etc. Other events which have evolved over the years are the Film Festival, and the tented Book Festival in Charlotte Square.

Open air events are held in Holyrood Park, and there are spectacular firework displays over the Castle. The Military Tattoo on the Castle Esplanade is a dazzling pageant of piping, dance and military display, and usually combines Scottish, British and overseas participants. For these events, and for the sake of visitors generally, Edinburgh citizens cross their fingers for some decent weather, which is by no means guaranteed.

The Edinburgh Festival is very important for the city's tourist industry. And tourism is now one of the most important and successful parts of the city's economy. Although more and more hotels have been built, it is still wise to book accommodation if you plan to visit Edinburgh during the Festival.

Edinburgh's Twin Cities Edinburgh today has eight 'twin' cities, with which it tries to maintain specially close civic links. The list of twin cities is as follows: Munich, Germany (linked since 1954); Nice, France (1958); Florence, Italy (1964); Dunedin, New Zealand (1974); San Diego, USA (1977); Xi'an, China (1985); Kiev, USSR (1989).

Edinburgh undergoes a personality change during the hectic Festival weeks. The atmosphere of the place seems to change. Yet for the rest of the year the city also leads something of a double life. From one view it is a professional, respectable place; from another, it suffers problems of unemployment, poor housing and poverty like any other city.

Every year there is a Festival Fringe poster competition for children, sponsored by the Life Association of Scotland.

People at Work

Tourism is now one of Edinburgh's biggest industries and employers. Witness the growing number of hotels and year-round facilities for visitors. The Edinburgh International Festival is only one reason for coming to Edinburgh. The city is also increasingly popular as a conference centre - people like to come to Edinburgh.

Education is not thought of as an industry, but Edinburgh employs above-average numbers of its citizens in the business of education. There are two large universities - Edinburgh (founded 1583) with its world famous teaching hospital and Royal College of Surgeons; and Heriot-Watt (1966) on its custom-built greenfield campus complete with technology park. There is also a dynamic polytechnic, a teacher training college, a variety of further education establishments and a wealth of schooling both public and private. Edinburgh is also home to the National Library of Scotland, the British Geological Survey, the astronomical observatories and the national museums.

It has long been a tradition in Edinburgh for its successful businessmen to bequeath some of their wealth to the establishment of schools. George Heriot (Jinglin Geordie), goldsmith to King James VI, James Gillespie, a snuff merchant and William Fettes, a wine and tea merchant, are examples.

George Heriot left money for the purchase of land and construction of a 'Hospital' for the maintenance and education of fatherless sons of Edinburgh burgesses. The original building is still in use today as a school.

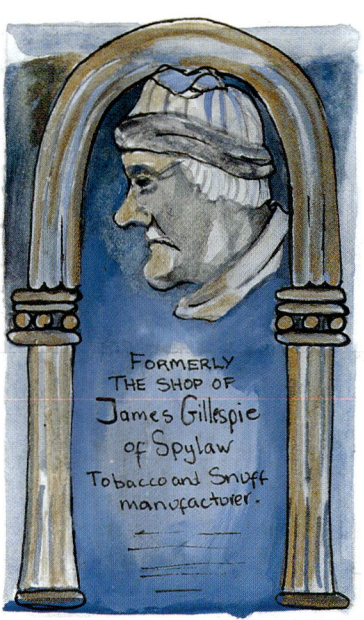

The James Gillespie plaque in the Royal Mile.

Finance and Banking. Nowadays Edinburgh claims to be the biggest financial centre in Europe outside the City of London. The Bank of Scotland and the Royal Bank of Scotland are both based here in splendid buildings, as are several large insurance companies. Then there are the investment and trust companies, many of them based in Charlotte Square and George Street, the stockbrokers, chartered accountants, and corporate lawyers - a compact and thriving network of money managers.

Industry. They used to say of Dundee that the main industries of that city were jam, jute and journalism. In Edinburgh it was beer, banks, books and biscuits. The banks are still here and the financial sector is flourishing. You can still smell the brewers at their work, though nowadays they nearly all work for the one large company. Most of the large publishing companies have either moved south or been taken over by multinationals, but a new generation of small companies has sprung up.

Biscuits - and confectionery - have mainly gone the way of books. But other industries have arrived - such as electronics, most notably in firms like Ferranti, Digital and Hewlett Packard.

Government. Edinburgh is home not only to the Scottish Office at St Andrew's House and its satellite departments located all over the city. It is also headquarters for the Lothian Regional Council and the Edinburgh District Council, so local government is also a large employer. And there are hopes of more government functions coming to the city.

Royal Bank of Scotland.

Edinburgh's City Chambers, originally the Royal Exchange building (1753), but taken over by the Town Council in 1811.

OUT AND ABOUT

There is a wealth of choice for activities in and around Edinburgh. Apart from the places already listed in the book, this is a further selection - all tried and tested - and not found to be wanting! If in doubt, telephone the place first. Have fun!

FOR ENERGETIC DAYS!

Braid Hills, South Edinburgh
Good for kites, walking and sledging, but watch out for golfers.
Bonaly Country Park, Edinburgh (031-445-3383)
On the northern slopes of the Pentlands. Woodland and hill walks, free fishing in Bonaly Reservoir.
Central Cycle Hire, 13 Lochrin Place, Tollcross (031-228-6333)
Mountain bikes a speciality.
Cramond Island, Cramond
At low tide you can walk out from Cramond foreshore over a rough causeway. Read the tide charts first!
Edinburgh Canal Centre, Ratho (031-333-1320)
Join either *Pride of the Union, Countess of Edinburgh* or the *Almond Queen* for a canal cruise. Visitor's Centre.
Hillend Ski Centre, Biggar Road
Biggest in Europe and one of the most modern. Wear protective clothing for the 'toothbrush' matting!
Kennedy's Fun Centre, 3 Windsor Place, Portobello (031-669-1075)
Indoor centre with trampolines.
Meadowbank Sports Centre, 139 London Road (031-661-5351)
Wide variety of sporting facilities.
Megabowl, Craig Park, Newcraighall Road (031-657-3731)
Cool cats go bowling here!
Murrayfield Ice Rink, Riversdale Crescent (031-337-6933)
Rink open at weekends from 10.00 and weekdays from 14.30.
Royal Commonwealth Pool, Dalkeith Road, (031-667-7211)
Largest covered flume complex in Europe. Try 'Black Vortex' if you dare! Olympic size pool, shallow teaching pool and diving pool.
(There are many other Edinburgh District Council pools - check for details on 031-667-7211 and ask for Dalry/Glenogle/Infirmary St./Portobello/Leith and Warrender.)
Silverknowes Riding Centre, Muirhouse Parkway (031-332-7777)
Tower Farm Riding Stables, Liberton (031-664-3475)
Wester Hailes Education Centre Pool (031-442-4217)
Large pool and children's pool. Floats session in the holidays.

Out of Town   *Almondell & Calderwood Country Park*, by Broxburn (0506-882254)
Nature trails, riverside and woodland walks.
Beecraigs Country Park, Linlithgow (0506-844516)
Woodland walks, deer and trout farms. Barbecue area. Trim course.
John Muir Country Park, nr. Dunbar
Conservation area with glorious beach, nature trail and woodland walks.
Maid of the Forth (031-331-1454)
Sail on the Forth and visit Inchcolm Island. (May-September.)
Inchcolm Abbey (031-244-3101)
On an island in the Forth - where they have held Festival productions of Macbeth.
Dalkeith Country Park (031-663-5684)
Adventure playground, woodland walks.
Vogrie Estate & Country Park (0875-21990)
Adventure playground 19 km south of Edinburgh. Nature trails and country walks. Open all year.
Flotterstone, Hillend Country Park
Walk up to the reservoirs and Pentland Hills.
Mariner Leisure Centre, Falkirk (0324-22083)
Tropical pool with wave machine and elephant chute.
Scottish Deer Centre, Cupar (023781-391)
Deer farm walk, adventure playground and nature trail. Open all year.
Yellowcraig Sands, Dirleton.
Beautiful beach and nature trail.

FOR QUIETER DAYS!

City Observatory, Calton Hill (031-556-4365)
'Edinburgh in Depth' is a full colour audio-visual experience which explores the turbulent history of Scotland's capital from its volcanic birth to the present day. March-October.
Royal Observatory, Blackford Hill (031-668-8100)
Visitor centre - a glimpse into the world of astronomy and space research.
Edinburgh Zoo, Corstorphine Road (031-334-9171)
See page 34. A great day out for all age ranges.
Gorgie City Farm, 51 Gorgie Road (031-337-4202)
See page 34. A close-up of many unusual farm animals.

Out of Town   *Bo'ness and Kinneil Railway*, Bo'ness (0506-822298)
A must for any railway steam buff. Train trips April-October.
Biggar Gasworks, Biggar (031-225-7534)
A unique monument - how coal gas was made. July-September. Afternoons only.
Gladstone Court Museum, Biggar (0899-21050)
A Street Museum. Wee shops and offices - as the old remember it! Easter-October 31. 10.00-12.30 and 14.00-17.00. Sun. 14.00-17.00.
Dalmeny House, 8 km west of Edinburgh (031-331-1888)
Family home of Earl of Rosebery. Woodland walks. Access by passenger ferry across River Almond at Cramond and by walking from South Queensferry.
Edinburgh Butterfly and Insect World, nr. Dalkeith (031-663-4932)
At Dobbie's Garden Centre. March-October. Wonderful to enjoy the tropical temperatures and see the exotic butterflies.
Hopetoun House, South Queensferry (031-331-2451)
Scotland's greatest Adam mansion set in acres of magnificent parkland. Famous paintings. Museum. Nature trail and Walled Garden Centre.
John Buchan Centre, Broughton (0899-21050)
Easter to mid-October. Daily 14.00-17.00.
Moat Park Heritage Centre, Biggar (0899-21050)
Displays of how the Clyde and Tweed valleys were formed, church, school and agricultural history. Easter-October 31. Mon.-Sat. 10.00-17.00. Sun. 14.00-17.00.
Museum of Flight, East Fortune (031-225-7534)
A fascinating collection of aircraft on a disused World War II airfield.
Myreton Motor Museum, by Aberlady (0857-57-288)
An interesting collection of cars, motor cycles etc.
St Andrews Sea Life Centre (0334-74786)
Overlooking West Sands Beach - discover a new world beneath the waves.
Scottish Fisheries Museum, Anstruther, Fife (0333-310628)
The many facets of fisher folklife are portrayed here, including whaling. Open all year.
Scottish Mining Museum, Lady Victoria Colliery, Newtongrange (031-663-7519)
A rare opportunity to visit an impressive colliery. Don your hard hat for the tour - all seen through the eyes of the people who worked and lived there.